The hatchback Elite of 1974 had a sharp-edged emphasis to the glass-fibre body style. Following current design trends, its headlamps folded away when not in use.

THE LOTUS

Graham Robson

Shire Publications Ltd

CONTENTS

Copyright © 1993 by Graham Robson. First published 1993. Shire Album 294. ISBN 0 7478 0217 3.

Printed in Great Britain by CIT Printing Services, Press Buildings, Merlins Bridge, Haverfordwest, Dyfed SA61 1XF.

British Library Cataloguing in Publication Data available.

Editorial Consultant: Michael E. Ware, Curator of the National Motor Museum, Beaulieu

ACKNOWLEDGEMENTS
The cover photograph is by Mirco Decet. Other illustrations are acknowledged as follows: *Autocar*, page 10 (bottom); Ford Motor Company, page 30 (bottom); National Motor Museum, pages 2, 3, 4 (bottom), 5 and 6; N. Wright/National Motor Museum, pages 4 (top) and 7 (bottom). The remainder are from the author's collection.

Cover: *Perhaps the most famous Lotus model of all time — the Esprit Turbo. It was introduced in 1980, the fastest car of its type in the world.*

Colin Chapman with Michael and Nigel Allen during the winter of 1950-1 designing the Lotus Mark II trials car. This car also had successes in speed trials and races.

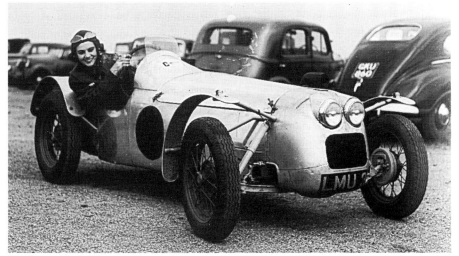

The Lotus Mark III was built to comply with the 750 Motor Club's racing formula for specials based on the Austin Seven. Chapman altered the inlet ports and this car was almost unbeatable during the 1951 season but his modifications were banned for the following season. Hazel Williams, later to become his wife, is seen driving the car.

COLIN CHAPMAN — RESTLESS GENIUS

Until a heart attack killed Colin Chapman, suddenly and at the tragically young age of 54, he *was* Lotus. For nearly thirty years he was founder, chairman, chief engineer, inspirational dynamo and presiding genius. Without Colin Chapman, Lotus would have collapsed on more than one occasion. In 1983, after he died, it nearly did.

Anthony Colin Bruce Chapman was born in Richmond, Surrey, in 1928 and was evacuated to Wisbech, in Cambridgeshire, during the Second World War but he returned to University College, London, in 1945 to study engineering. Then and always, Chapman was fanatically interested in cars, and for the first few years after the war he tried to make money by buying and selling old bangers.

By this stage he had met Hazel Williams, who was to become his wife, and had learned to tide over his regular financial crises by borrowing money from her father. In 1948 he graduated as a civil engineer specialising in structural engineering and then joined the RAF on a short-term commission and learned to fly.

His love affair with flying never palled, but he soon became disenchanted with the RAF, so in 1949 he resigned his commission and eventually went to work for the British Aluminium Company, where he had to convince possible industrial customers that structural aluminium was the right choice for roof extensions.

For Chapman this job was merely a means of earning his living, but he had already started to build special cars when he could find the time and was soon spending as much time in a workshop in the evenings as he was on his official job during the day.

The very first Lotus car — a one-off trials special based on a 1930 Austin Seven and later called the Mark I — took shape in 1948 in the workshop at the side of the house of his father, Vic Chapman, in London N2. It was soon followed by the Mark II, a trials car which was later raced, and the Mark III, which was a 750 Formula race car.

The Mark VI Lotus was designed officially to take the 1508 cc Ford Consul engine, but shortage of engines from Ford caused people to look elsewhere for power units. One of the most successful Mark VI drivers was Peter Gammon, who used a 1467 cc MG-powered car, seen here at Castle Combe in 1954.

The Lotus Seven was conceived as a road- and track-going sports car. Many were used on the roads on weekdays and raced at weekends. Here H. D. Kilburn lets his Lotus Seven Series 2 get out of control while coming out of the chicane at Goodwood.

A typical enthusiastic club racer, sprint and hill-climb exponent, John Barnes from Selsey, with his Lotus Seven at Goodwood in 1961.

By this time, although the British Aluminium Company paid his salary, Chapman was becoming totally involved in racing and racing-car design. The Mark III featured not only tubular frame stiffening to the Austin Seven chassis, but a carefully thought-out way of tuning the engine.

In 1952 he took the big step of setting up a company, the Lotus Engineering Company, whose premises were an old stable which his father owned at Tottenham Lane, Hornsey, in north London, and it was typical of Chapman that he took a loan of £25 from Hazel to help him get started. His partner was Michael Allen, the arrangement being that Allen would work full-time in the business and Chapman would devote all his spare time to it, while continuing to work with British Aluminium. There were no other employees, and Hazel Chapman dealt with the paperwork.

Business was brisk, not only in building up specials but also in manufacturing components, and before long Chapman decided that it was time to start building cars in numbers.

The first series-production Lotus, therefore, was called the Mark VI and went on sale in 1953. Assembled almost entirely in the cramped and crudely equipped premises in Hornsey, the Mark VI was a starkly styled two-seater sports car with a multi-tubular chassis frame (usually described as a 'space frame', because it was three-dimensional and surrounded, rather than supported, the engine and transmission) and exposed front wheels. Lotus, however, was not large enough to build its own bodies. These were produced by Williams & Pritchard of Edmonton, and the engines and gearboxes were lightly modified Ford products, most of the cars having heavy Ford Consul four-cylinder units. To avoid the necessity for purchase tax to be charged (this was nearly twenty years before value added tax was imposed in Britain), Lotus supplied the Mark VI in kit form, and the customer sometimes arranged to buy and fit his own engine and transmission.

Even though the layout of the Mark VI was crude by later Lotus standards, it was a car which appealed to the many enthu-

Many different engines could be fitted to the Lotus Seven, particularly the Ford 100E 1172 cc, the BMC A type and 948 cc or 1098 cc, and the Ford Anglia 997 cc. The Super Seven offered the 1500 cc Ford in various states of tune. When competing in a hill-climb at Prescott, David Embley gets the Semicircle wrong in his Ford-engined Seven.

siasts who wanted to build and race their own sports cars. It was such a simple kit, too, that they could build it in the garage at home. Demand was brisk and, even though there was still only a tiny workforce at Lotus, the business boomed. In three years no fewer than 110 such cars were built.

Although the VI was not a pretty car, it was small, lightweight and purposeful, with great agility on the race track, and many class successes were achieved by private owners.

During the 1950s the Lotus business boomed. Not only was the VI replaced by the Seven (a car which is still being made today, in much modified form, by Caterham Cars as the Caterham Seven), but it was soon joined by sleeker and more specialised racing cars. The Seven, though, was a completely new approach, in detail, to the design of a small, square-rig, two-seater sports car, where function took precedence over style, and where comfort was of minor importance.

It has often been stated that the Seven

is more of a 'four-wheel motorcycle' than a car, not only in the precise way that it handled, but in the way that it never allowed comfort, space and relaxed motoring to get in the way of its prime purpose — which was to go very quickly indeed. 25 years after the Seven was originally put on sale the Caterham version was more popular than ever before, with more than five hundred being built every year. In that period the basic chassis design was never changed, although in Caterham's hands the cockpit was made more spacious and an ever wider range of engines was offered. There was one odd period, between 1969 and 1973, when a Mark IV version was produced, with a glass-fibre body shell, but all the 'classic' Sevens, including the later Caterhams, have light alloy bodies and what can best be described as skimpy bad-weather protection.

In that time an enormous variety of proprietary four-cylinder engines were made available. Under Lotus control (to 1973) these varied between the 40 bhp

6

In the first few years Lotus produced spindly two-seater sports cars with multi-tube chassis frames. The design of the famous Seven was sold to Caterham Cars in the 1970s and was reborn as the Caterham Super Seven.

Prince Edward with Lord Montagu in the 1992 Caterham Super Seven. This car was offered as first prize in a raffle run by the National Motor Museum at Beaulieu to celebrate its fortieth anniversary.

side-valve Ford 100E unit of 1.2 litres and the 125 bhp twin-cam Lotus-Ford unit of 1.6 litres. As with the Mark VI, the Seven was an ideal kit car, on which purchase tax was not imposed, but soon after the introduction of VAT in 1973 Colin Chapman sold the production rights to Caterham Cars of Surrey, one of his dealers. Well over three thousand Lotus-badged Sevens were produced in fifteen years, but Caterham production has now exceeded that figure.

To supplement the Seven, a whole series of streamlined two-seater sports cars changed the face of British sports-car racing. In 1957 Lotus produced its first single-seater racing car, and the move into Grand Prix racing followed almost immediately afterwards.

Not only did Chapman's racing cars have streamlined, wind-cheating shapes, but they also had ultra-light multi-tube chassis, long travel and supple suspension, and were usually lighter than all their competitors. As racing cars they were enormously effective, though they also gained a reputation for fragility.

In those days Lotus attracted great characters on to its staff, including Mike Costin as the chief development engineer, his brother Frank as aerodynamic consultant, Graham Hill as mechanic and racing driver, and Keith Duckworth as transmission development engineer. Wages were rarely generous and working hours were long but Chapman managed to generate enormous loyalty to his company and to himself.

By the late 1950s, however, Chapman's ambitions had outgrown his scruffy little factory in Hornsey, for he wanted to turn Lotus into a manufacturer of real road cars. The breakthrough came with the Elite — and a move to Cheshunt.

From 1962 Lotus began to build cars with its own design of engine. This had a twin overhead-camshaft head grafted on to the bottom end of a Ford unit and was usually backed by a Ford gearbox.

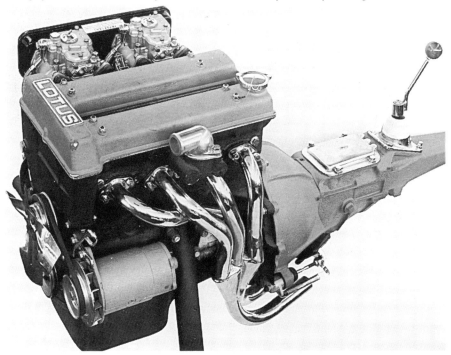

For the first true Lotus road car, Colin Chapman designed a unit-construction glass-fibre coupé, calling it the Elite. On sale from 1959 to 1963, it was powered by a Coventry-Climax engine.

CHESHUNT DAYS: ELITE, ELAN, PLUS TWO, EUROPA

Colin Chapman saw Lotus come of age in the 1960s, with not one but two new factories, with amazingly successful Grand Prix cars beating the world's best, and with the launch of a stream of new road-car models. It was also the period in which the business was floated on the stock market and in which the company's founder officially became a millionaire.

Lotus's expansion to become a builder of true road cars came in 1957-9. In the beginning, all Lotus sports cars had been meant for racing but some of them could be used on the road. By the late 1950s, however, Colin Chapman's ambitions were boundless: he decided it was time for him to design a dedicated road-going sports car, and the result was the original Elite.

Like many other Lotus cars over the years, the Elite was technically adventurous. Some firms were already producing unit-construction cars (that is, cars with no separate chassis frame) and others were using moulded glass-fibre bodywork. Against all advice, Chapman, the lateral thinker, decided to become the first to combine the two technologies to make the car as light as possible.

Although the new car was previewed in 1957, there was not enough floor space to manufacture the new two-seater Elite coupé at Hornsey, so in 1959 Lotus moved into a brand-new factory in Delamare Road, Cheshunt, Hertfordshire. Straight away, though, Lotus encountered a problem which would recur repeatedly in future years: the Elite cost too much to make. Lotus had to underprice the Elite to sell enough, but this made it unprofitable. If the price had been raised, sales would have dwindled disastrously.

The new Coventry-Climax engined car, therefore, may have looked stunning and had high performance with good fuel economy but it had to be subsidised by the sale of racing cars. Fortunately this was not a problem at the time, for Lotus had begun making successful mid-engined single-seaters, while in the Formula One team Jim Clark was well on the way to becoming World Champion.

In 1962, however, Chapman found the secret to commercial success by forming a grand alliance with Ford which involved racing cars, a new engine and a new range of cars. He began by building

The long-running Elan series was announced in 1962 and was produced for twelve years. All types were tiny glass-fibre bodied two-seaters, some with open tops and some with this smart coupé roof. This is a Series 4 version.

The 1962 Elan was the first Lotus to use a steel backbone chassis frame, a construction Lotus has retained into the 1990s.

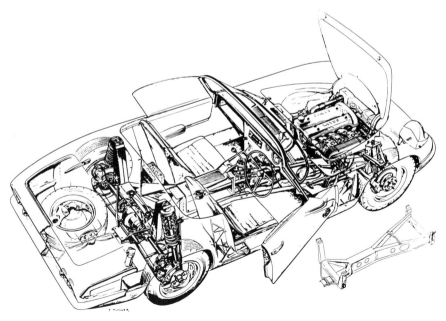

Lotus's first major co-operative venture was to assemble the Ford Lotus-Cortina at Cheshunt on behalf of Ford. In production from 1963 to 1966, it was a famously successful racing and rally car.

Ford-engined racing cars for Ford-USA, but the crucial commercial move was to design a new 1.5 litre twin-camshaft road-car engine around the bare bones of a Ford-UK unit.

The new engine was vital to Ford and to Lotus interests. Ford needed it to power an ultra-fast version of the new Cortina, while Lotus needed it to use in entirely new sports cars to be called Elan and Elan Plus Two. Not only was this engine as powerful as the Elite's Coventry-Climax unit, but it was much cheaper to build.

The first of the Ford-powered Lotuses was the tiny little Elan two-seater sports car of 1962, which was the first Lotus to use a steel backbone type of frame. When Ford also invited Lotus to assemble its new high-performance car (titled Lotus-Cortina) at Cheshunt from 1963, Colin Chapman's future looked assured. From being a company which was struggling for survival, Lotus became extremely profitable, and its cars sold well.

Only about one thousand road cars were built at Cheshunt in 1963, but this rocketed to 2500 cars in 1966. In only four years, therefore, Cheshunt came to burst at the seams, and Lotus's pre-tax profits soared to more than £250,000 a year. Yet another factory move seemed to be inevitable, so Chapman and his advisors looked around, spreading their search even further, and selected a disused USAF bomber airfield at Hethel, just a few miles southwest of Norwich.

Because Lotus-Cortina assembly ended in 1966, the move to a brand-new factory complex, started in 1966 and completed by the end of the following year, allowed two new types of road car to be introduced. The Elan Plus Two was a coupé, still with the Lotus-Ford engine, but considerably larger than the Elan, for it had a longer wheelbase, a wider track and 2+2 seating.

11

The Lotus Elan Plus 2 of the late 1960s was a longer, wider, 2+2 version of the Lotus Elan, only ever built as a fixed-head coupé. In the background is the garage block of Colin Chapman's Norfolk house, East Carleton Hall.

The Elan Plus Two was the first 2+2 seater car produced by Lotus and was meant to be a completely habitable sports coupé, with more accommodation than the original Elan.

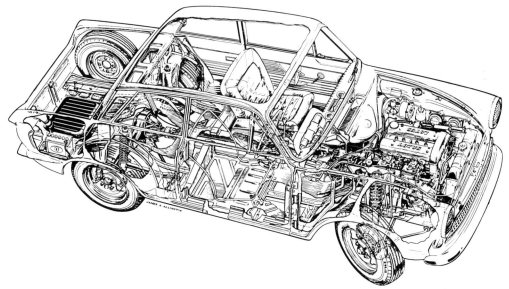

The original Lotus-Cortina used a two-door Ford Cortina body shell but was powered by the modern Lotus-Ford twin-cam engine and had a unique rear suspension layout.

The other new car, called Europa, was yet another imaginative project. Colin Chapman decided to produce a mid-engined two-seater (with the engine mounted behind the seats) at a lower price than the Elan, but to do this he needed to buy in complete engine and transmission units. In a far-sighted deal he joined forces with Renault of France, who provided Renault 16TS hardware and also helped to distribute the cars in Europe for the first two years.

By 1968, when Lotus prepared to become a public company and sell its shares on the stock market, the company was making more than three thousand cars a year and announced pre-tax profits of £731,000. Because it was the first to use the famous Ford-Cosworth DFV Formula One engine, the Grand Prix team was the most successful in the world and there were more big plans for company expansion.

Hethel was ideal for this thrusting young company, for there was ample space for new factory buildings to be erected alongside the perimeter track, which formed a test track literally on the doorstep, and the local authorities were delighted to give all possible help to generate new jobs. Chapman himself, who had been awarded the CBE, had built himself a magnificent Regency-style house a few miles away. He could indulge his love of flying by basing the company aeroplane at Hethel itself and was revelling in the progress of his Grand Prix team. For more reasons than one he was often known as the 'Businessman of the Decade'.

Because his company now had a great deal of financial muscle (Hethel and its atmosphere seemed to be bigger, glossier and light years away from the cramped days at Hornsey, although there was only a decade between them), Chapman planned to take Lotus even further up-market in the 1970s. He wanted to get out of the kit-car business, and he wanted to produce a series of Lotus cars that were larger and faster than ever before.

The mid-engined Lotus Europa was revealed in 1966, with a backbone frame, a GRP body and a Renault engine. Later types, like this Europa Special, used the Lotus-Ford engine.

The mid-engined Europa was a two-seater, pure and simple, with the steel backbone frame separating the seats, and with the engine immediately behind the passengers' heads.

The second-generation Ford Lotus-Cortina, of 1967-70, had a similar body platform to the original type, but it was assembled by Ford at Dagenham.

Lotus's founder, Colin Chapman, and his wife, Hazel, pulling the first pint of beer at Pub Lotus, in London.

Tony Rudd, affectionately known as 'Uncle Tony', joined Lotus from BRM in 1969, to direct all new engine design and development work. As Group Technical Director, he retired in 1991.

In the mid 1970s Lotus's engine-building department was working overtime, producing sixteen-valve units for itself and for use in the Jensen-Healey.

James Bond drives out of the sea in his submersible Esprit in the film 'The Spy Who Loved Me'. It may have been a fake, but the publicity value was tremendous.

THE 1970S HETHEL GENERATION: ELITE, EXCEL, ESPRIT

By 1970 Chapman's master plan was taking shape. Kit-car production was wound down, a completely new design of sixteen-valve twin-cam engine was unveiled, and a distinguished engineer, Tony Rudd, joined the company from BRM to look after all engine developments. It took longer than expected for Group Lotus Car Companies Ltd (the name of the new public company) to develop two new model families, but in the meantime Chapman negotiated a major deal, to supply the new engines for Jensen to use in the Jensen-Healey sports car; this contract lasted from 1972 to 1976, with nearly 11,000 engines eventually supplied.

At the same time the Grand Prix team was once again dominant in Formula One, with the wedge-style Type 72 (Jochen Rindt became World Champion in 1970, and Emerson Fittipaldi took over in 1972), so Lotus's name seemed to crop up everywhere. There seemed to be plenty of life left in the existing road cars too. Rudd oversaw the development of more powerful (126 bhp) 'big valve' engines which were offered in the front-engined cars from 1970, and a young man called Mike Kimberley arrived to run the development project which replaced the Europa's Renault engine with the Lotus-Ford unit.

Great Britain joined the European Community in 1973 and this had one immediate effect on the motor industry. VAT replaced purchase tax, and kit cars could no longer be supplied tax-free. Fortunately, Lotus had almost abandoned that business by then. A bigger blow came at the end of the year, when the first energy crisis crippled car sales in many markets.

Lotus, which had made pre-tax profits of £1.16 million in 1973, found its sales rapidly declining and it was a great relief to all concerned when the first new-generation Lotus, a front-engined four-seater hatchback called the Elite, went on sale. Except for the five-speed gearbox, the new Elite had nothing in common with the old-type Elans.

Compared with the Elan Plus Two, the Elite was longer, wider, larger, heavier — and much more expensive. The last of the Elans cost £3486 and the existing 5.3 litre Jaguar E-Type cost £3812, but prices of the new Elite started at £5445 — and a number of expensive options could be added to raise that even higher.

In some ways this was a familiar new

Lotus — it had a backbone frame and a glass-fibre body — but in others it was startlingly modern. It was the first ever Lotus to use the new sixteen-valve engine, and the first and only Lotus to have a hatchback style. On the other hand, it had typical Lotus-like performance and roadholding.

Only 687 Elites were built in 1974, which was the high-point of that car's appeal, but a conventional fastback coupé derivative, the Eclat, was soon added and sales stabilised at that level for the rest of the decade.

By 1976, though, these modern cars had been completely overshadowed by the launch of the most sensational Lotus road car of all — the Esprit. Like the old Europa, which was discontinued in 1975, this exciting creation was a mid-engined machine with a backbone chassis, but it used the modern sixteen-valve engine and a five-speed Citroën gearbox and it featured a startlingly attractive body style by the Italian master Giorgetto Giugiaro.

Everyone — Lotus managers, motoring writers and the customers — seemed to love the Esprit, which was exactly what they all thought a 1970s Lotus needed to be. It was a beautiful car with a very effective chassis; it steered, handled and rode in an exemplary manner and, considering that it was a 2 litre car, it was astonishingly fast.

On the other hand, a great deal of investment had been needed to introduce two major new models in two years, which explains why Lotus's finances slumped to a £488,000 loss in 1975, recovering to a profit of £556,700 in 1977. Even so, by the end of the decade a big and lucrative assembly deal with Talbot (to produce the Lotus-engined Talbot Sunbeam-Lotus) had been clinched, a major design and

Lotus designed this new sixteen-valve twin-cam four-cylinder engine to power all its 1970s products, front-engined or mid-engined. It was still being developed, and improved, in the early 1990s.

Earlier Lotus cars were small, even cramped, little two-seaters, but the Elite and its Eclat/ Excel relatives were genuine close-coupled four-seaters.

Foldaway headlamps make the daytime style of this mid-1970s Elite look sleek, but at night the aerodynamics of the car are ruined.

The fastback Eclat coupé was derived from the hatchback Elite. This basic coupé style would be used continuously at Hethel until the early 1990s.

One of Lotus's most successful contract jobs was to install its own engine into this car, the Talbot Sunbeam-Lotus, and then to build all the production cars between 1979 and 1981.

development programme with DeLorean was under way, and a turbocharged Esprit was being planned. Mike Kimberley had become Lotus's managing director, allowing Colin Chapman to spend more of his time with Team Lotus, the Formula One racing team.

For the moment Lotus's path seemed secure, even though the profit figures did not always back this. In 1980 the sixteen-valve engines were enlarged to 2.2 litres and the 210 bhp Esprit Turbo went on sale, while profits soared to £1.28 million. The following year DeLorean's Lotus-designed car finally went on sale in a cloud of hype — yet only 383 Lotus cars were produced in 1981, and profits dropped to £461,000.

Even though Lotus built the twenty-thousandth sixteen-valve engine in the autumn of 1981 and prices were slashed in an attempt to boost sales, the future looked bleak for a time. Lotus, surely, could not survive in recession-hit Britain without finding a larger protective industrial partner? At this time, however, Colin Chapman pulled off a master stroke, by forging links with Toyota of Japan. The immediate result of this deal was that Toyota provided components to allow the Eclat to become the Excel, but in the longer term Toyota would take a share

stake, and work would also begin on a new small Toyota-engined Lotus.

At the end of 1982 the hatchback Elite was dropped, the Excel replaced the Eclat at a significantly lower price, and all looked set fair. Then came a shattering blow. In the last few months Chapman had been under considerable stress but had never showed this. Everyone considered him to be immortal, with a bottomless reserve of energy and spirit. Suddenly, on 16th December, having returned from an acrimonious FISA Formula One meeting in France, he collapsed and died of a heart attack.

Because Chapman had been not only chairman but also the inspiration of the business and a major shareholder, for a few days the company drifted helplessly. Then, in short order, Toyota took a share stake, loans owed to American Express were repaid and the finance director, Fred Bushell, became Lotus's chairman.

It was a dark time for everyone connected with Lotus, but the company never looked like closing. Perhaps it was all summed up by the Latin inscription engraved on Colin Chapman's tombstone at East Carleton church: *Crescit sub pondere virtus*. In translation this means: 'In adversity we thrive.' Chapman himself would have approved.

To replace the long-running Europa, Lotus devised a new and larger chassis, used the sixteen-valve Type 907 engine and commissioned this remarkable style from Giugiaro for the Esprit model.

When the mid-engined Esprit went on sale in 1976, it was a rather cramped two-seater, where the seats, the fascia and the centre tunnel were all wrapped closely round the passengers.

The Esprit was a dramatically styled, low-to-the-ground road-burner with unmistakable looks.

The Esprit S3 arrived in 1981, with a much-modified chassis to add to the 160 bhp 2.2 litre engine. It had a top speed of 135 mph (217 km/h).

Lotus kept on improving the Esprit design. In 1980 the engine was enlarged from 2.0 litres to 2.2 litres without upsetting the balance of the design.

More publicity for the early 1980s! Goodyear sponsored the Formula One team and the new Esprit Turbo featured in the film 'For Your Eyes Only'.

Pound for pound, or inch for inch, the turbocharged Lotus engine of 1980 was probably the most efficient in the world. The 2.2 litre unit produced 210 bhp, and the Esprit's top speed was nearly 150 mph (240 km/h).

Soon after Lotus forged a strategic alliance with Toyota of Japan in 1981, the Eclat chassis was redeveloped as the Excel, with a Toyota gearbox and rear axle. The rugged backbone chassis was retained.

Lotus's 1980s road cars were luxuriously equipped: this was the new Excel of 1982.

The early 1980s Lotus Excel was a slightly smoothed-out version of the Eclat, a 160 bhp 130 mph (210 km/h) four-seater with impressive roadholding.

In 1987 Lotus introduced a completely restyled Esprit design, whose more rounded body hid the same type of mid-engined chassis. This car is the 264 bhp Turbo SE of 1989.

FRONT-WHEEL-DRIVE ELAN: A 1990S SPORTS CAR

If Lotus had a long-term strategy in the early 1980s, it was rarely obvious to observers. Perhaps the business did not drift, but it had to spend much of its time fighting off crisis after crisis. Time-wasting projects like the boat business and the development of microlight aircraft engines had to be wound up as soon as possible, while the long-term financing of the companys had to be stabilised. The Formula One team went through a difficult period and the much-rumoured V8 road-car engine was shown but then cancelled.

On top of all this, the simmering financial scandal surrounding the DeLorean business, and Colin Chapman's part in the diversion of funds, finally boiled over. In normal circumstances it was difficult enough for Lotus to look forward, but with receivers, tax inspectors and Fraud Squad officers swarming around the place life was almost impossible.

Also, out of the public eye, there was the on-going problem of the 'new Elan', a new car which changed with the seasons. Before he died, Colin Chapman's strategy in joining forces with Toyota had been to develop a new, smaller and cheaper sports car, which would use Toyota's modern engines and transmissions. That was in 1981 but it would be eight years before a radically different 'new Elan' would go on the market.

Meanwhile Lotus rapidly built up its consultancy and contract engineering business. It developed its own V8 and V12 engines, as well as a turbocharged 1.5 litre V6 Grand Prix engine for Toyota. This produced 1000 bhp but the project was cancelled. Lotus developed a new engine for Chrysler, sorted out the suspension of Isuzu's Piazza, developed a turbocharged engine for the BL Metro, worked continuously on an 'active suspension' installation of its own and seemed to have a number of satisfied clients all around the world.

By 1985 David Wickins, chairman of British Car Auctions, had become Lotus's chairman, with BCA, Toyota and JCB, the construction machinery company, all having major shareholdings. New factory buildings had been erected, the company, if not its late founder, had been cleared of any involvement in the continuing DeLorean scandal and the business was

Mike Kimberley joined Lotus as a development engineer in 1969, became its chief executive before the end of the 1970s and guided Lotus safely into the ownership of General Motors during the 1980s.

expanding rapidly. Esprit and Excel sales continued steadily, but the aim was to get the 'new Elan' into production and increase Lotus's output to five thousand cars a year.

Then, in January 1986, the world's largest car-making conglomerate, General Motors of the United States, made a £22.75 million takeover bid for Lotus. The main shareholders agreed to the terms and within days the business had become a GM subsidiary. Alan Curtis, who became chairman, and Mike Kimberley, the chief executive, both expressed delight, for Lotus's long-term future was now assured. At a stroke Lotus not only had the backing of all the capital it needed, but it could also provide engineering consultancy to massive companies like GM in the USA, Isuzu of Japan, Vauxhall and Opel. Such work started immediately, one of the first results being the launch of the Lotus-designed four-cam 5.7 litre engine for the Chevrolet.

In April 1987 Lotus also acquired the big Millbrook proving-ground complex in Bedfordshire, which had originally been built for Vauxhall to use, and later that year a completely rebodied mid-engined Esprit was launched. The turbocharged version of that car would soon become even more powerful — and with 264 bhp this was the most efficient 2.2 litre engine in the world. In 1988 work began on a 'super-saloon' project for Vauxhall-Opel, and in 1989 the company announced that this new car, the Vauxhall Lotus-Carlton/Opel Lotus-Omega, would be assembled at Hethel.

For the long term, though, Lotus planned to press ahead with the new Elan project, the car with which it intended to change and expand its market. When this eventually appeared, in 1989, it had had a long and complex history.

The controversial front-wheel-drive Elan sports car went on sale in 1989 but production was stopped in 1992 when Lotus's masters, General Motors, decided that it would never be profitable.

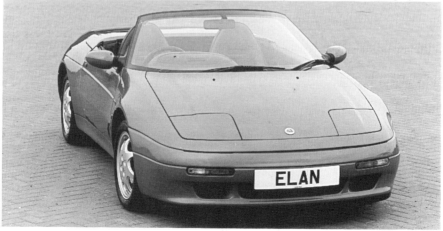

Like earlier saloon cars which Lotus had transformed, the Vauxhall Lotus-Carlton of 1990 was a miraculously faster version of the Carlton, with a much more powerful engine. In this case 377 bhp guaranteed a top speed of 176 mph (283 km/h).

The first 'new Elan' was the M90 of 1981-4, a front-engine, rear-drive Toyota-powered car with a 1.6 litre engine, but by 1985 this had been killed off in favour of the X100 project, a radically new front-wheel-drive Toyota-engined two-seater which used Corolla running gear. Immediately after the GM takeover, however, X100 was cancelled, and Mike Kimberley then approved work on M100, which was still a front-wheel-drive car, but this time it was to use an Isuzu (of Japan) 1.6 litre engine and transmission pack in a curvaceous, stubby and wide two-seater body.

The M100 was one of the most widely leaked projects in Lotus's history, so when it was launched as the new-generation Elan in October 1989 the layout was already familiar to every enthusiast. This, Lotus forecast, was a new type of sports car which would sell in larger numbers, and most observers agreed that it was probably the best-handling front-wheel-drive car in the world.

Unfortunately, although it was technically miraculous, the new Elan was financially disastrous. Well before sales began it was promoted as 'the £15,000 Lotus' but the turbocharged version actually went on sale at £19,850 and in the USA it was listed at nearly $40,000. Sales were disappointing in the United Kingdom, and well below expectations in the United States.

Even though these prices were disappointingly high, Lotus could make no profit from the car, as it discovered that the new Elan was probably as expensive to build as the previous-generation Esprits and Excels. The Elan, therefore, completed a short and eventful career in July 1992, when GM instructed Lotus to cease production after only 3855 had been made. At the same time the old Excel was also discontinued.

The company put a brave face on the latest crisis and promised more 'supercar' developments in the future. For the next few years, though, Lotus would have to survive by building limited numbers of re-engined (and cheapened) Esprits, by completing the 1100 production run of Lotus-Carlton saloons, and by its very profitable consultancy business.

Even so, old hands were quite relaxed about all this. Lotus had been in trouble before and had always bounced back. The bounce of the mid 1990s, they forecast, would be exciting to behold.

THE DELOREAN CONNECTION

John DeLorean was an American who had been a high-ranking executive with General Motors in the 1960s and 1970s. He conceived a rear-engined sports coupé for sale to customers in the USA. He was aiming to dominate what might be called the 'Porsche 911 market' but lacked the engineers to make his car roadworthy. Colin Chapman and Lotus were hired to accomplish this and were remarkably successful.

At first sight this was a simple contract job which Lotus completed efficiently. But rarely can a project which started out so proudly have ended in such ignominy. Lotus was justly proud of the work it did in turning John DeLorean's impractical dream into a practical motor car, but no one could be proud of the huge losses, the fraud and the financial embezzlement which followed.

John DeLorean's dream car was conceived in 1974, as a rear-engined (not mid-engined, as sometimes stated) two-seater sports coupé, which would have lift-up 'gull-wing' doors and stainless steel skin panels. Giorgetto Giugiaro, who was then working on the Lotus Esprit style, produced the shape, which, at the time, was intended to have a plastic composite structure. DeLorean's problem was that he had nowhere to build the car, and no suitable engine and transmission to power it. Four years later, DeLorean had chosen the Renault 30's 2.85 litre V6 engine and transmission but had been refused financial aid to build a factory in Puerto Rico or in the Republic of Ireland. Finally he persuaded the British government to back him in Northern Ireland. Lotus was then hired to turn the dream into reality.

The British government-funded project was unsuccessful and ultimately cost the British taxpayer a great deal of money, for in the end the DeLorean car was not easy to sell. Lotus, however, deserve credit for making something of it, for the design, which had been ridiculously under-developed in 1978, was ready for sale in 1981. It was not Lotus's fault that the American public did not share John DeLorean's vision: faced with the demand to make a rear-engined two-seater coupé practical, Lotus achieved precisely that.

At first DeLorean wanted the job completed in eighteen months, which was out of the question, and in the end he settled for about 25 months. In that time Lotus re-engineered the car to use an Esprit type of backbone frame and a glass-reinforced plastic (GRP) body skeleton under the stainless steel panels; Giugiaro was asked to restyle the shape, and a completely new factory was erected at Dunmurry, near Belfast.

Lotus became so involved in this project that many domestic projects (like the turbocharged Esprit) had to be delayed until engineers were available once again. The first DeLorean DMC-12 production cars were eventually built at Dunmurry in January 1981 and the first shipment to the USA followed in June of that year.

At first DeLorean publicists boasted that DeLoreans were in short supply and that customers were fighting to take deliveries. By November 1981 eighty DMC-12s were being built every day, but by that time the car's reputation had collapsed. Road-test reports had been disappointing — the car was nothing like as fast as had been hoped; there were major quality problems, and the price was seen as much too high.

The end was swift but messy. The British government refused to supply any more funds to tide over the business in Northern Ireland, the receivers were called in during February 1982, and the last DMC-12 of all was built later in that year.

For the motoring magazines the story was over, but for Fleet Street it was only just beginning. It was not until after Colin Chapman's death in 1982 that the DeLorean project changed from a fiasco into a financial scandal.

Jim Clark smokes his way off the starting grid in a Lotus 25 of 1963, on his way to the World Championship of that year.

FAMOUS FORMULA ONE LOTUSES

Once Colin Chapman had established Lotus as a small-scale maker of road cars, he built up a works team which began to race special machines throughout Europe. Almost immediately he inspired the design of advanced, ultra-lightweight and carefully streamlined sports cars.

At this period, in the 1950s, Chapman himself designed the cars' structure, while the aerodynamicist Frank Costin shaped the astonishing low-drag bodies. Since Lotus could not afford its own engines or transmissions, these were always bought in from outside suppliers, notably from Coventry-Climax of Coventry.

Until 1966 every Lotus racing car used a Coventry-Climax engine. The first Lotus single-seater racing car was the Mark 12 of 1957, a front-engined Formula Two machine which was soon given a more powerful engine to compete in Formula One events, and the following year the beauti-

fully streamlined Mark 16 was introduced. Then came the first mid-engined Lotus, the 18 of 1960, a 240 bhp car in which Stirling Moss won the Monaco Grand Prix in 1960, thus starting a long series of Lotus victories which continued into the 1980s.

Since then there have been many famous, and some less successful, Formula One Lotuses. The most successful have been the 25, 49, 72, 78, 97 and 98.

The Lotus 25 was the world's first single-seater to have a monocoque structure. It used a 200 bhp 1.5 litre V8 Coventry-Climax engine. This car and the 33, which was developed from it, gave Jim Clark two World Championships in 1963 and 1965.

The Lotus 49 was the first car to use the famous 3 litre Ford-Cosworth DFV V8 engine, which produced more than 400 bhp. It won many Formula One races between 1967 and 1969 and in 1968 Graham Hill became World Champion in this car.

29

The Lotus 49 was the first Formula One car to use the Ford-Cosworth DFV engine. By 1969 Graham Hill had used it to become World Champion, and the aerodynamic age had arrived.

The Lotus 72 was another Cosworth DFV-engined car, the familiar 'wedge-shaped' Lotus. Jochen Rindt won the World Championship in it in 1970, and Emerson Fittipaldi did so in 1972.

The Lotus 78 was the first 'ground-effect' Formula One car, still with Cosworth DFV power, and producing 500 bhp. Mario Andretti drove it to become World Champion in 1977.

The Lotus 97 and Lotus 98 were the V6 turbocharged Renault 1.5 litre cars, with at least 800 bhp, in which Ayrton Senna started winning Formula One races in 1985 and 1986.

Four personalities closely connected with Lotus and its success, pictured in 1967: (left to right) Keith Duckworth, Cosworth engine designer; Graham Hill, racing driver; Colin Chapman, the founder; and Harley Copp, Ford's technical chief.

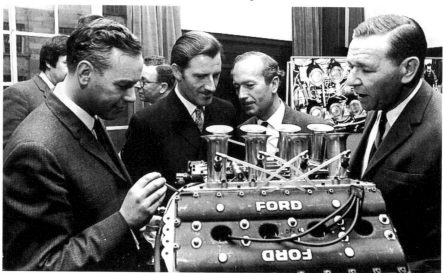

Jochen Rindt became Grand Prix racing's World Champion in 1970 in this wedge-styled Lotus 72.

Ayrton Senna led the Lotus Formula One team in the 1985-7 period. In 1986, using the Renault turbo-powered Lotus 98, Senna finished fourth in the Drivers' Championship.

FURTHER READING

A number of other books have been published on the subject of Lotus. The following is a selection of the most valuable volumes concerning the cars and the company.

Bolster, John. *The Lotus Elan and Europa*. Motor Racing Publications, 1980.
Coulter, Jeremy. *The Lotus and Caterham Sevens*. Motor Racing Publications, 1986.
Crombac, Gerard 'Jabby'. *Colin Chapman: The Man and His Cars*. Patrick Stephens, 1986.
Hughes, Mark. *Lotus Elan*. Osprey Automotive, 1992.
Nye, Doug. *The Story of Lotus 1961—1971*. Motor Racing Publications, 1972 and 1978.
Nye, Doug. *Theme Lotus, from Chapman to Decarouge*. Motor Racing Publications, 1978 and 1986.
Robson, Graham. *Lotus since the 1970s* (two volumes). Motor Racing Publications, 1993.
Smith, Ian H. *The Story of Lotus 1947—1960*. Motor Racing Publications, 1970 and 1982.

PLACES TO VISIT

Some notable British motor museums and collections are listed below. Although none specialises in Lotus sports cars, examples of various types are usually on display. If you intend to make a visit, it is advisable to discover the times of opening before you make a special journey, and to check that the cars which interest you are still on display.

The Donington Collection, Donington Park, Castle Donington, Derby DE7 2RP. Telephone: 0332 810048.

Haynes Sparkford Motor Museum, Sparkford, Yeovil, Somerset BA22 7LH. Telephone: 0963 40804.

Midland Motor Museum, Stanmore Hall, Stourbridge Road, Bridgnorth, Shropshire WV15 6DT. Telephone: 0746 761761.

Museum of British Road Transport, St Agnes Lane, Hales Street, Coventry, West Midlands CV1 1PN. Telephone: 0203 832425.

National Motor Museum, John Montagu Building, Beaulieu, Brockenhurst, Hampshire SO42 7ZN. Telephone: 0590 612345.

The Patrick Collection, 180 Lifford Lane, King's Norton, Birmingham, West Midlands B30 3NT. Telephone: 021-459 9111.

Totnes Motor Museum, Steamer Quay, Totnes, Devon TQ9 5AL. Telephone: 0803 862777.